What bird has a head like this?

A great horned owl!

This owl is named for the two "horns" on top of its head, even though they are actually bunches of feathers. Like all owls, the great horned owl can turn its head right around to look directly behind it — in both directions. And *whooo* might it be searching for? Its prey (animals it eats), which includes mice, rabbits and sometimes even raccoons.

What bird has
a **beak** like this?

A hummingbird!

This hummingbird's long, thin beak might look like a straw, but it isn't used for sucking up liquids. The beak is perfectly shaped for reaching into tube-shaped flowers so the tiny bird can use its long *tongue* to collect nectar. As well, the lower part of the hummingbird's beak is flexible, which is helpful for snapping up the insects it also eats.

What bird has eyes like this?

A bald eagle!

A bald eagle's eyesight is six times more powerful than a human's! It can also see in front and to the side *at the same time.* This bird of prey (one that hunts for its food) can use its sharp eyesight to focus on its next meal — often a moving target. such as a swimming fish — from hundreds of feet above before swooping down for the catch.

What bird has a body like this?

A kiwi!

A kiwi's pear-shaped body is built for living close to the ground, not up in the air. This flightless bird's wings are so small that they are hard to see, and its bushy, hair-like feathers have markings that help it blend in with the growth on the forest floor where it lives. Most birds have light, hollow bones and a tail to make flying easier, but the kiwi has heavy bones and no tail.

What bird has
wings like this?

An arctic tern!

This mighty flier is a world champion when it comes to migration (a journey from one home to another). Each year. an arctic tern flies from the Arctic to the Antarctic ... and then all the way back again! Its long. narrow wings are perfectly suited for gliding and soaring — when it isn't flapping its wings. it is saving much-needed energy. In fact. a tern is so good at gliding. it can glide in its sleep!

What bird has legs like this?

A flamingo!

A flamingo's stilt-like legs are perfect for wading. Having long legs means the flamingo can go into deeper water to find more of the food it eats, such as plant-like algae and tiny brine shrimp. But when a flamingo rests or even sleeps, it often balances atop just one leg. Its joints lock into place to keep one leg tucked — sometimes for hours at a time!

What bird has
feet like this?

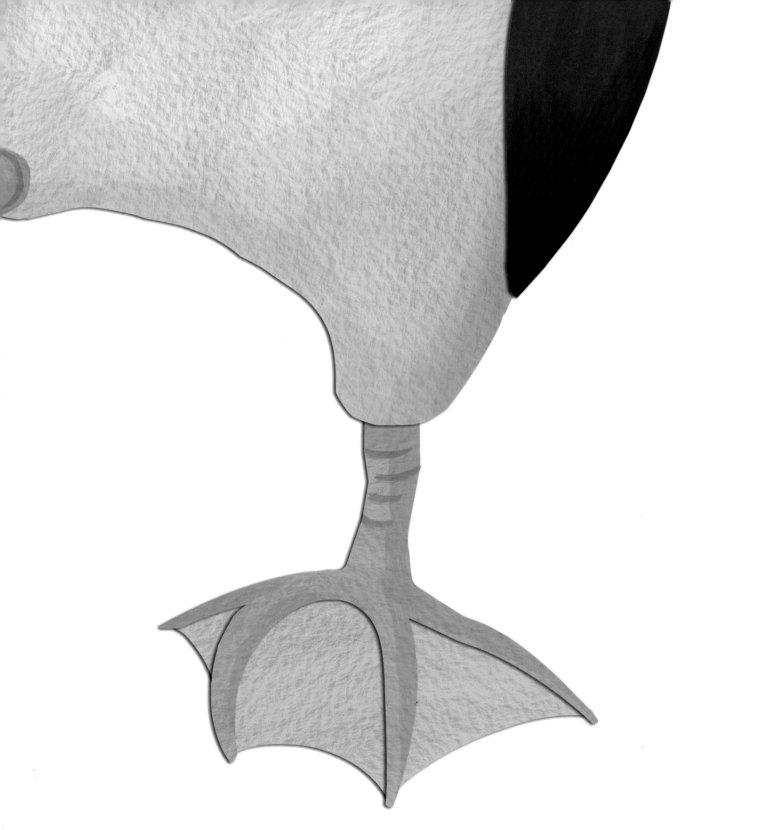

A blue-footed booby!

To impress a female during mating season
(the time of year for having babies), a male
blue-footed booby performs a strutting
dance, slowly raising one foot at a time. Both
males and females look for a partner with the
bluest feet. That's because the birds with the
brightest-colored feet are the healthiest.

What bird has
a tail like this?

A peacock!

When a peacock fans out his colorful tail,
it is all about showing off. During mating
season, this male bird displays his shimmery
feathers with "eye" markings to attract
the attention of a female, called a peahen.
Once this season is over, the peacock's long
tail feathers fall out ... only to grow back
again the next year.

Other Awesome Birds

A turkey vulture's red head is featherless so its food (rotting meat!) doesn't stick to it.

A parrot uses its hard, curved beak to crack seeds and nutshells.

An ostrich's eyeball is bigger than its brain.

A thick layer of fat called blubber helps a penguin's body stay warm.

The wandering albatross has the longest wingspan of any living bird.

A ruffed grouse's leg feathers help keep it warm in the winter.

When cracking open a nut to eat, a blue jay holds it with its foot.

While pecking for insects, a woodpecker uses its stiff tail to steady itself against the tree trunk.

For Owen, the little birdie who suggested I write this book — S.R.

To Imin and Jared, for helping me find my song when the dawn was still dark — K.M.

Acknowledgments

Many thanks to biologist Emily Rondel of Bird Studies Canada and Mark Peck, Ornithology Technician, Royal Ontario Museum, for generously sharing their time and expertise to review this manuscript. Any errors that may have crept in along the way are solely mine. And, of course, much gratitude to all the good eggs at KCP, with special thanks to Olga Kidisevic, Yvette Ghione, Julia Naimska and Katie Scott. Finally, an enormous thank you to Kwanchai Moriya for making this book truly soar with his beautiful illustrations.

Text © 2018 Stacey Roderick
Illustrations © 2018 Kwanchai Moriya

Kids Can Press gratefully acknowledges the financial support of the Government of Ontario, through the Ontario Media Development Corporation; the Ontario Arts Council; the Canada Council for the Arts; and the Government of Canada, through the CBF, for our publishing activity.

Published in Canada and the U.S. by Kids Can Press Ltd.
25 Dockside Drive, Toronto, ON M5A 0B5

Kids Can Press is a Corus Entertainment Inc. company

www.kidscanpress.com

The artwork in this book was created in Adobe Photoshop and Illustrator, using original photographs and textures.

The text is set in Squidtoonz.

Edited by Katie Scott
Designed by Julia Naimska

Printed and bound in Shenzhen, China, in 3/2018 by Imago

CM 18 0 9 8 7 6 5 4 3 2 1

Library and Archives Canada Cataloguing in Publication

Roderick, Stacey, author
   Birds from head to tail / written by Stacey Roderick : illustrated by Kwanchai Moriya.

(Head to tail)
ISBN 978-1-77138-925-9 (hardcover)

   1. Birds — Juvenile literature. I. Moriya, Kwanchai, illustrator
II. Title.

QL676.2.R64 2018   j598   C2017-906643-9

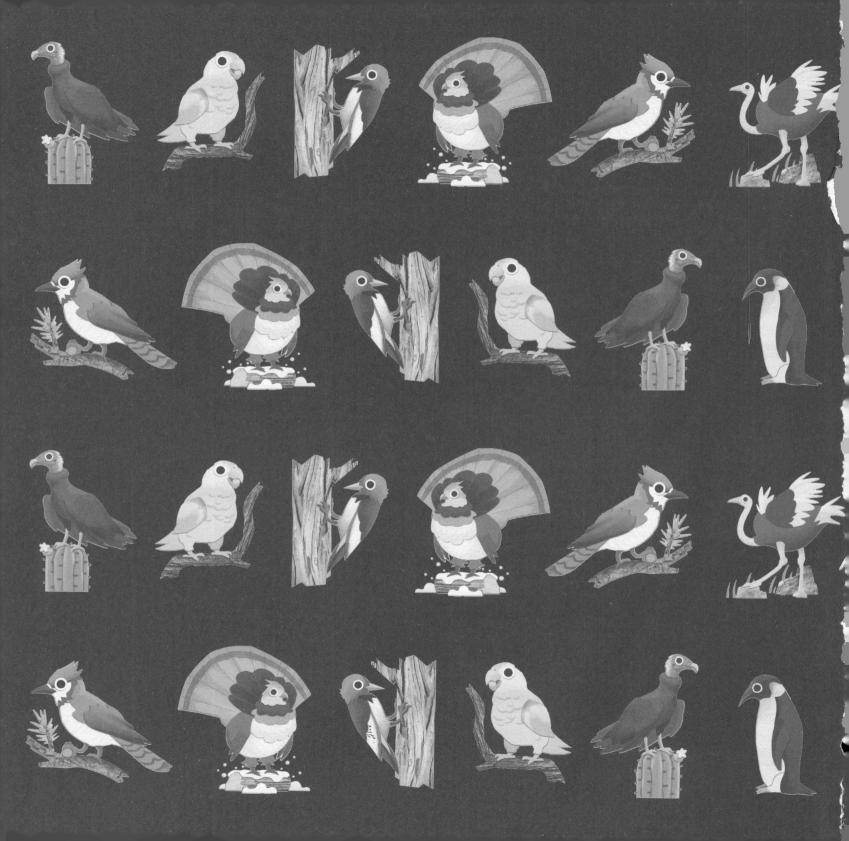